MILITARY SERVICE

CAREERS IN THE
U.S. ARMY

MILITARY SERVICE

CAREERS IN THE
U.S. ARMY

BY EDWARD F. DOLAN

mc Marshall Cavendish
Benchmark
New York

Special thanks to West Point graduate
LTC Mark D. Brigham (retired) of the U.S. Army.

MARSHALL CAVENDISH BENCHMARK
99 WHITE PLAINS ROAD
TARRYTOWN, NY 10591
www.marshallcavendish.us

Copyright © 2010 by Marshall Cavendish Corporation

All rights reserved. No part of this book may be reproduced or utilized in any form or by
any means electronic or mechanical, including photocopying, recording, or by any information storage and retrieval system, without permission from the copyright holders.

All Internet sites were available and accurate when this book was sent to press.

Library of Congress Cataloging-in-Publication Data

Dolan, Edward F., 1924–
Careers in the U.S. Army / by Edward F. Dolan.
p. cm. — (Military service)
Includes bibliographical references and index.
Summary: "Discusses service in the U.S. Army, including training, educational benefits, and
career opportunities"—Provided by publisher.
ISBN 978-0-7614-4206-6
1. United States. Army—Vocational guidance. I. Title.
UB323.D65 2008
355.0023'73—dc22
2008027821

EDITOR: Megan Comerford PUBLISHER: Michelle Bisson
ART DIRECTOR: Anahid Hamparian SERIES DESIGNER: Kristen Branch / Michael Nelson Design

Photo research by Candlepants Incorporated
Cover photo: Pvt. Brandi Marshall / U.S. Army Photo
The photographs in this book are used by permission and through the courtesy of:
U.S. Army Photo: 7; Staff Sgt. Rebekah-Mae Bruns, 16; Tom Mani, 21; Cheresa D. Theiral, 24;
Spc. Clint Stein, 29; Tech. Sgt. Roger M. Dey, 31; Tech. Sgt. Denise Rayder, 44; Staff Sgt. Reeba
Critser, 48, 74-75; Senior Airman Brian Ferguson, 51; Spc. Ben Brody, 56; Lucille Anne
Newman, 58; Sgt. 1st Class Gail Braymen, 64-65; Lt. Col. William Thurmond, 69; Petty Officer
1st Class Martin Anton Edgil, 10-11; Spc. Jeremy Crisp, 26-27; Sgt. Paula Taylor, 54-55. *New
York Public Library*: Print Collection, Miriam and Ira D. Wallach Division of Art, Prints and
Photographs, 13. *AP Images*: 36; New Mexico State University, Darren Phillips, 71; Las Cruces
Sun-News, Norm Dettlaff, 73. *Air Force Staff Sgt. Derrick C. Goode*: 47. *Department of Defense*:
2-3, 14-15, 32-33, 38-39, 40-41, 66-67, back cover.

Printed in Malaysia
1 3 5 6 4 2

CONTENTS

INTRODUCTION
THE BIRTH OF AN ARMY   6

ONE
BRANCHES OF THE ARMY   10

TWO
WAYS TO SERVE IN THE ARMY   26

THREE
STARTING LIFE IN UNIFORM   40

FOUR
THE CHAIN OF COMMAND   54

FIVE
SALARY AND BENEFITS   66

ACRONYM GLOSSARY   76
FURTHER INFORMATION   77
INDEX   78

INTRODUCTION

THE BIRTH OF AN ARMY

The Continental army was formed on June 14, 1775, two months after the Revolutionary War began. The Continental Congress put General George Washington in command of the new force, which fought the eight-year-long war against the British for independence.

Though the Continental army, which was formed of local militias, struggled at first, American troops were ultimately victorious. The British surrendered at Yorktown, Virginia, in October 1781. The thirteen colonies—officially free from British rule with the signing of the Treaty of Paris in 1783—became the United States of America. The end of the war also resulted in Washington's resignation as Commander in Chief, and the Continental army was disbanded. Congress rejected Washington's proposals to maintain a national military force.

SGT Donald Chatman takes aim during a dime-and-washer exercise at the Warrior Training Course. The exercise evaluates the skill of a soldier's trigger squeeze. A dime (or washer) is placed on the barrel of the rifle. The soldier must fire six consecutive shots from an unsupported position without allowing the dime to fall.

CAREERS IN THE U.S. ARMY

The new nation was quickly spreading westward, and settlers often faced opposition from the native American Indian tribes. Despite the states' initial hesitations about forming a standing army, people soon realized that the informal state militias were not sufficient defense. The nation needed a force of formally trained soldiers.

In the late 1780s the states ratified the U.S. Constitution, which enabled the federal government to establish an army. Shortly thereafter the United States Army was formed. It was placed under the command of the U.S. Department of War, which was renamed the Department of the Army, a division of the U.S. Department of Defense, in 1947.

Today, over two hundred years later, more than one million men and women serve in the U.S. Army, the world's best-equipped military force. It is a force that is divided into three main groups: the active-duty Army, the Army Reserve, and the National Guard. As of 2009, more than 494,000 men and women served on active duty. Another 246,000 were in the Army Reserve, while 325,000 were members of the National Guard. There are more than 140 areas of specialization for an active-duty soldier, many of which are available to part-time soldiers, too.

This book is aimed primarily at young men and women who are thinking of joining the U.S. Army. One reader may feel it is his or her patriotic duty. Another might wish to serve to honor the memory of a loved one or friend killed or injured in action. One person may see the Army as a career.

THE BIRTH OF AN ARMY

Another may see the Army as the first step on the road to a university degree or the source of the technical training needed for future civilian work. Still others may join for the oldest reason of all: the desire to meet new people and see faraway places.

Time spent in the Army, no matter how long, brings rewards. It provides training and a sense of discipline that are useful in civilian life. The academic and practical experience men and women receive in a variety of technical, administrative, and service areas are respected assets in both military and civilian careers. Former members of the military are increasingly sought by civilian employers.

The U.S. Army has quite a lot to offer.

ONE

BRANCHES OF THE ARMY

THE U.S. ARMY IS DIVIDED INTO AREAS called branches that provide the personnel, equipment, and services needed for the Army to function successfully. There are basic branches, where most soldiers serve, and special branches, which require special training, military experience, and degrees of higher education. Everyone—man and woman, private soldier, noncommissioned officer, warrant officer, and commissioned officer—is assigned to one of these branches according to his or her military occupational specialty (MOS).

THE BRANCHES OF THE ARMY

Basic branches are further organized into three interdependent categories: Combat Arms, Combat Support Arms, and Combat Service Support. The

The twenty-first century conflict in the Middle East has involved many soldiers from the U.S. Army. Here, members of the 2nd Infantry Division are on a reconnaissance mission in Baghdad in 2006.

CAREERS IN THE U.S. ARMY

Combat Arms branches, such as the Infantry, engage in combat. Those branches are assisted by Combat Support Arms branches that provide necessary support including weapons and ammunition, communication facilities, engineering projects, and intelligence services; the Military Intelligence Corps functions as combat support. The Combat Service Support units, such as the Transportation Corps, make sure that all troops are well manned, armed, fed, clothed, and moved quickly to wherever they are needed.

COMBAT ARMS BRANCHES

ARMY AVIATION Army Aviation maintains and operates aircraft essential to the operation of ground forces. Its principal aircraft today is the helicopter. The branch deposits troops in combat areas, withdraws them when necessary, evacuates the wounded, and provides fire support for ground troops.

AIR DEFENSE ARTILLERY Air Defense units are equipped with antiaircraft missiles used to defend both military and civilian installations. The branch has adapted to the increasing threat that air and missile attacks pose in the twenty-first century. Most officers and crewmembers are specially trained in at least one of the major systems: the PATRIOT missile system, the Bradley linebacker system, the man portable air defense system (MANPADS), or the AVENGER system.

THE FIRST DRILL INSTRUCTOR

One of the most important figures in the Revolutionary War was Baron Friedrich Wilhelm von Steuben, an unemployed professional soldier from Prussia. He traveled to America in late 1777 after Benjamin Franklin wrote to General George Washington on his behalf. Von Steuben reported to Washington in February 1778 and offered his services while the American troops were struggling through the brutal winter at Valley Forge, Pennsylvania.

The newcomer quickly became an invaluable addition to Washington's staff. The American troops were competent marksmen and willing to fight, but they had no formal military training. Von Steuben immediately started training them in battle tactics and the effective use of their muskets and bayonets.

He started by instructing small groups of men, who then went on to coach small groups of their own. Von Steuben did not speak English and used translators to give instructions. During his drill sessions, von Steuben swore at the soldiers in German, French, and English. By the end of the winter, the Americans were better prepared to face the well-trained British troops.

In addition to instructing the men, von Steuben wrote an infantry training manual that the Army used for decades after the Revolution. For his work, von Steuben, who never returned to Europe after the Revolution, is known as the Father of the American Army.

Above: Baron von Steuben was responsible for turning the American militia into a formidable army during the Revolutionary War.

CAREERS IN THE U.S. ARMY

ARMOR   The Armor branch includes armored and cavalry units and is responsible for battlefield reconnaissance missions. Armor crewmen operate equipment and fire weapons to destroy enemy positions, including the 61-ton (55-metric ton) M1A2 Abrams main battle tank—the chief combat tank for armor troops in both the Army and the Marine Corps. Other equipment in the Armor branch include the M113 tracked vehicles and the Stryker, a versatile wheeled vehicle.

CORPS OF ENGINEERS   The Corps of Engineers works on both military and civilian projects ranging from minefield emplacement to the construction of bridges and buildings. The corps also works with natural resources and provides battlefield support. There are combat, construction, and topographic specialties within the corps.

BRANCHES OF THE ARMY

The howitzer is a common artillery piece. In Afghanistan, soldiers from 3rd Battalion, 7th Field Artillery Regiment, 25th Infantry Division (Light), were part of a unit that won the 2005 Phoenix Award for outstanding duty.

CAREERS IN THE U.S. ARMY

FIELD ARTILLERY Artillery are large, mounted firearms used for discharging missiles and are generally manned by multi-soldier crews. The Field Artillery branch of the Army is in charge of all ground operations that require artillery pieces, including howitzers, mortars, and antiaircraft artillery. In the late twentieth century, artillery pieces, which had been manually aimed and discharged, were equipped with artillery computer systems (ACS) to enable precision firing.

The M16 rifle is the first weapon introduced to soldiers during basic training and is the main personal weapon for soldiers, particularly those in infantry units. The M16 can be fitted with a grenade launcher or a scope, such as the one used by this solider with the 7th Infantry Division to provide cover as his comrades raid a building in Iraq.

BRANCHES OF THE ARMY

INFANTRY The Infantry is not only the oldest but also the most fundamental of the Army's combat forces. Its basic task is to attack and engage the enemy on the ground, aiming to seize enemy territory. The M16A2 assault rifle is the standard-issue weapon for infantrymen; fully loaded, it weighs only 8.79 pounds (4 kg). An M16 can be fired from the hip or shoulder while standing, kneeling, or lying facedown. It can be set for automatic fire of three-round bursts or semiautomatic fire of single bursts. There is also an attachment that makes the rifle an M203 grenade launcher.

Today, women are not permitted to serve as combat infantry soldiers, though they may—and do—serve with support units in combat zones. There is, however, a growing demand for change, with a number of political figures urging that combat roles be made open to women as a means of giving them full citizenship rights and responsibilities.

COMBAT SUPPORT ARMS

CHEMICAL CORPS Soldiers with the Chemical Corps study nuclear, biological, and chemical (NBC) weapons. The corps can detect and identify NBC agents; conduct decontamination operations; and develop, store, and employ NBC weapons. The research done by the Chemical Corps keeps soldiers prepared for potential nuclear, biological, or chemical attacks. Chemical operations specialists prepare emergency procedures in the event of a biological attack.

CAREERS IN THE U.S. ARMY

MILITARY INTELLIGENCE CORPS Military Intelligence (MI) collects and analyzes information important to military operations and to the nation's security. Though MI personnel have been a part of the Army since the eighteenth century, the corps was not formed until 1967. Officers in MI assess the risk of planned actions and work to neutralize intelligence threats. MI soldiers often specialize in a specific area of intelligence systems or data, such as human intelligence or electronic warfare. Imagery intelligence collects and analyzes optical, infrared, and radar images while counterintelligence focuses on enemy intelligence operations. The MI motto is "Always Out Front" because the corps is out collecting information before any military action is taken.

MILITARY POLICE CORPS Founded in 1941, the Military Police (MP) Corps fulfills duties that range from traffic control in both peace- and wartime to the supervision of prisoners of war. The corps functions as the Army's own law enforcement agency. MPs provide security on base and in the field, respond to criminal acts and emergencies, enforce military laws and regulations, and conduct police intelligence operations.

SIGNAL CORPS The Signal Corps provides and manages communications and information systems support for the Army and for joint operations. The corps enables troops to communicate and exchange data securely and in real time

BRANCHES OF THE ARMY

through networks that use satellites, video-teleconferencing, radios, computers, and other systems. Soldiers with the Signal Corps specialize in either information systems operations, signal (communications) operations, or visual information operations. Though signals have been used by the Army since the Revolutionary War—including the lanterns that set Paul Revere on his midnight ride—the Signal Corps was not officially established until 1860. Since then, the corps has progressed from "wigwag" flag messages to the telegraph to the complex technology of today.

COMBAT SERVICE SUPPORT

ADJUTANT GENERAL CORPS The Adjutant General Corps is the human resources department of the Army and is in charge of managing personnel. Officers assist the unit commanders by keeping troops prepared for combat, organizing and distributing information, and helping to maintain the well-being of the soldiers. Men and women with the Adjutant General Corps are trained in the Army's protocol in areas including casualty operations, information management, postal operations, and morale, welfare, and recreation support.

FINANCE CORPS The Finance Corps attends to a wide variety of money matters, from the dispersal of salaries to troops to the payment of bills from outside suppliers. Soldiers with the corps are trained to organize commercial

CAREERS IN THE U.S. ARMY

vendor vouchers, account for the disbursement of public funds, and prepare travel funds. The Finance Corps is important in meeting the logistical, medical, and supply requirements of tactical missions.

ORDNANCE CORPS To keep its reputation as the world's best-equipped army, the U.S. Army must maintain a wide range of weapons systems, collectively called "ordnance." The Ordnance Corps ensures that the Army's weapons systems, vehicles, and equipment are always ready and available. The corps contracts with private firms for the purchase, production, and storage of arms; sets production standards for the suppliers; and provides the government with data on costs. Soldiers with the corps are able to maintain and repair not only weapons and vehicles, but also air conditioners, bath units, and water purifiers. The Ordnance Corps offers its soldiers certification opportunities from technical agencies, including the American Welding Society and the Automotive Society of Excellence.

QUARTERMASTER CORPS The Quartermaster Corps is the nation's oldest Combat Service Support branch. It provides troops with logistics support, supplying rations, clothing, supplies, and equipment. Everything from fresh water in the desert to petroleum for military vehicles is provided by the Quartermaster. As the corps' mission statement asserts, the corps delivers the correct supplies in the quantity

BRANCHES OF THE ARMY

Military police provide security not only on bases, but also at Army events. SGT Hardenio Abdon and his canine partner, Rex, were policing the entrance to the twenty-first annual Army Ten Miler race in Washington, DC.

WEAPONS TERMINOLOGY

automatic A firearm that automatically extracts and ejects the fired cartridge case and then loads a new one. A fully automatic firearm continues to load and fire when the trigger is pressed until there is no more ammunition. A semiautomatic firearm discharges one shot per trigger-pull.

barrel The tubular part of a firearm through which the bullet or projectile travels when the weapon is fired.

caliber The diameter of the inside of a gun barrel. The measurements are sometimes given in millimeters, abbreviated as mm, and sometimes in inches, abbreviated as cal, which is short for caliber. Guns and cartridges are designated by their caliber (9 mm handgun, .50 cal rifle).

cannon A large, heavy, tube-shaped artillery piece that launches a projectile.

carbine A firearm similar to a rifle, but shorter and not as powerful.

cartridge A tube containing a charge and a bullet for one ammunition round.

machine gun A mounted automatic firearm designed to fire cartridges in quick succession.

magazine A holder in or on a firearm that holds the cartridges to be fed into the gun's chamber.

missile A self-propelled explosive projectile.

mortar A muzzle-loading, short-range cannon that fires shells at high angles.

muzzle The end of a firearm that discharges ammunition.

pistol A handgun.

rifle A long-barreled firearm designed to be fired from the shoulder. The interior of the barrel is grooved, or "rifled."

BRANCHES OF THE ARMY

needed at the correct time and place, thus enabling troops to be successful in the field.

TRANSPORTATION CORPS The Transportation Corps handles the movement of personnel, supplies, and equipment to wherever they are needed in times of war or peace. All forms of transport—motor vehicles, trains, ships, and aircraft—are used. The corps also takes advantage of facilities such as pipelines and aerial tramways located in combat zones to move soldiers and materiel. The efficient movement and delivery of troops are essential to the Army's success.

THE SPECIAL BRANCHES

ARMY MEDICAL DEPARTMENT (AMEDD) The Army provides health care to all its soldiers and their families. Included in the Army health care system are the Medical Corps, the Army Nurse Corps, the Army Dental Corps, the Veterinary Corps, the Medical Service Corps, and the Army Medical Specialist Corps. Doctors, nurses, and medical staff work at bases both in the United States and overseas, as well as in the field during wartime and for disaster relief.

CHAPLAINS CORPS The Chaplains Corps consists of representatives of the Protestant, Catholic, Jewish, and Islamic faiths. They conduct religious services and provide counseling, morale enhancement, and other support to soldiers and their families.

CAREERS IN THE U.S. ARMY

JUDGE ADVOCATE GENERAL'S CORPS   The Judge Advocate General's Corp (JAG) handles legal matters for the Army and its soldiers, from contracts with civilian companies to courts-martial for soldiers of every rank. Soldiers with JAG also serve as prosecutors and defense attorneys in criminal trials.

SPECIAL OPERATIONS FORCES   Not all soldiers fight in traditional ways. Some are members of the Army Special

Soldiers in ARSOF units undergo intense physical and mental training. PFC John Swankie crosses a rope bridge during training with the Readiness Enhancement Company of the 19th Special Forces Group (Airborne).

BRANCHES OF THE ARMY

Operations Forces (ARSOF), such as Special Forces (nicknamed the Green Berets), Delta Force, and the Army Rangers. Unlike regular infantrymen, special operations units are trained and equipped for unconventional warfare. ARSOF operations are conducted both in peace- and wartime by twelve-man teams and have national military, political, economic, or psychological objectives. Units use stealth, surprise, and speed to do their job, usually operating deep inside enemy territory, striking with guerilla attacks, carrying out acts of sabotage, or gathering reconnaissance material, and then departing as swiftly and silently as they arrived. In addition, they often help train foreign troops and guerilla fighters to better protect their lands. Finally, Special Operations soldiers usually have about ten years of military service already completed. This gives them the experience and maturity vital to their success.

WAYS TO SERVE IN THE ARMY

TWO

THERE ARE FIVE WAYS TO SERVE IN THE U.S. Army: by enlisting in the active-duty Army; by joining the Army Reserve, the National Guard, or the Reserve Officers Training Corps (ROTC); or as a graduate from the U.S. Military Academy at West Point in New York. A West Point graduate enters the Army as a commissioned lieutenant. Everyone who wishes to serve must meet certain requirements.

- They must be U.S. citizens or meet noncitizen requirements.
- They must be between the ages of seventeen and thirty-four; those who are seventeen need parental consent.
- They must be high school graduates or have a high school equivalency diploma.

Three infantrymen from the Illinois National Guard search for insurgents in Abu Ghraib, Iraq. Soldiers always work in groups, never alone.

CAREERS IN THE U.S. ARMY

Enlistees must also pass urinalysis tests for drug and alcohol abuse and must meet a variety of legal and medical standards.

ON ACTIVE DUTY WITH THE ARMY

Active-duty service with the Army is a full-time job that can lead to a life-long career. Soldiers can sign up for two- to six-year terms of enlistment and may be posted either in the United States or overseas. As of 2009 there were more than 494,000 men and women on active duty with the Army.

Every soldier begins his or her career in the Army with basic combat training (BCT), followed by advanced individual training (AIT), which prepares soldiers for work in their specialties. After the training period is complete, soldiers are officially privates in the Army and are assigned to their first duty stations.

At the end of an enlistment term, soldiers may also decide to leave the Army or join a Reserve or National Guard unit. A soldier who wants to build a career in the Army must maintain active-duty service and advance through the ranks. After twenty years of service soldiers are eligible for retirement.

U.S. ARMY RESERVE

The Army Reserve originated out of the Medical Reserve Corps, which was established by Congress in 1908 so the

WAYS TO SERVE IN THE ARMY

Forty-six soldiers reenlist before a playoff game between the Denver Broncos and the New England Patriots at Mile High Stadium in Colorado. Both full-time and part-time soldiers can reenlist if they wish to continue their service.

CAREERS IN THE U.S. ARMY

country would have a reserve unit of trained officers. The unit was expanded in 1916, and again in 1920, to include both officers and enlisted personnel under the Organized Reserve Corps, which was renamed the Army Reserve in 1952. Reserve troops have served in nearly every major war and combat zone since World War I. They are also called to active duty to provide support and aid during national emergencies.

The Army Reserve trains its members so they are capable of serving a range of active-duty operations during either peace or war. Like active-duty soldiers, reservists must undergo BCT and AIT. Most of the areas available for specialization in the regular Army are also available to reservists.

A reservist must participate in drill and work sessions at least one weekend each month and attend an annual two-week training period. Men and women without previous military service are required to sign up for eight years; those who have already served with any branch of the military can enlist for periods of two to six years.

Soldiers within a mobilized Reserve unit are paid full-time active-duty salaries that vary according to rank. Under federal law, two years is the maximum period of time that a reservist can be kept on active duty. Under most circumstances the law also requires the reservist's civilian employer to give a returning soldier his or her former job, or an equivalent position. The reservist must have notified his or her employer of the call to duty and must return immediately to work.

WAYS TO SERVE IN THE ARMY

NATIONAL GUARD

The United States National Guard, which became the Army's primary reserve force in 1916, is made up of units that are committed to protecting their home states in times of crisis—such as natural disasters or civil upheavals—and to defending the nation and its interests worldwide. The National Guard itself is divided into two units: the Army National Guard (ARNG)

Oregon National Guardsmen PVT Michael Brown and SGT Nathan Bodle search through the flooded streets of northern New Orleans, Louisiana, looking for people stranded after Hurricane Rita. National Guard units provide relief to areas struck by natural disasters.

CAREERS IN THE U.S. ARMY

and the Air National Guard (ANG).

Service with the ARNG is similar to that with the Reserve. Members are expected to participate in a monthly weekend drill and an annual two-week training period. After BCT every member of the National Guard is assigned a combat, support, or administrative MOS, and is paid a part-time salary.

ARNG units can also be called to active duty by Congress during times of war or emergency. During active duty an ARNG member's pay increases to that of a full-time soldier at his or her rank. Like with the Army Reserve, there is a federal two-year active-duty service maximum and civilian job security for men and women with the National Guard.

RESERVE OFFICERS TRAINING CORPS

The Army's Reserve Officers Training Corps (ROTC) was founded by Congress in 1862. It is an instructional program, offered at colleges and universities, that trains young men and women to serve as commissioned officers in the U.S. Army. The Navy, which includes the Marine Corps, and the Air Force also sponsor ROTC programs.

WAYS TO SERVE IN THE ARMY

Lindsey Rowland is a cadet with the University of Hawaii's ROTC program. She is throwing a grenade as part of a competition between ROTC squads from Alaska, Hawaii, and Guam.

CAREERS IN THE U.S. ARMY

ROTC programs differ little in essentials from place to place. The program has three basic requirements: wear the ROTC uniform once a week, participate in unit drill instruction at least once a week, and attend an Army service course each semester. Cadets receive instruction in military leadership, Army traditions, military tactics, and communication. Otherwise, ROTC students live much as their fellow students do.

In addition, the ROTC cadet must complete a regular college course load for a bachelor's degree; studies must include calculus, calculus-based physics, English grammar and composition, and a course in national security policy and American military affairs.

Students can enroll in the ROTC Basic Course, which takes about two years to complete, without committing to military service; they are not commissioned. However, cadets who receive a ROTC scholarship or who enroll in the advanced course are obligated to fulfill a period of service after graduation. The Army also offers the four-week Leader's Training Course and the Leader Development Course for those who want further leadership training.

The ROTC program offers scholarships to assist its students. The scholarships, which are awarded based on merit and not need, provide full tuition, funds for textbooks and uniforms, and a stipend. They are granted for two- and four-year terms.

WAYS TO SERVE IN THE ARMY

A cadet is commissioned as a second lieutenant after completing his or her ROTC studies; the new officer is obligated to complete eight years of military service—four years on active duty and four years on Reserve duty, after which he or she may make a career as an Army officer or become a member of the Reserve.

U.S. MILITARY ACADEMY

The U.S. Military Academy at West Point, New York, was established in 1802 after both George Washington and Thomas Jefferson recognized the need for a school to train officers in the newly founded army. West Point, which was originally a colonial supply depot during the Revolutionary War, became the first military academy in the nation and attracted men from all the former colonies.

During its first decades West Point concentrated on producing engineers. Graduates won widespread praise for their work constructing dams, waterways, harbor facilities, and most of the nation's railroad lines prior to the Civil War. The academy has since expanded to offer majors in more than forty disciplines.

Today, West Point is a highly selective undergraduate school that admits approximately 1,200 men and women— and graduates 25 percent of the Army's new lieutenants— each year. Over the years West Point has expanded its curriculum to put increasing emphasis on the humanities,

Colin Powell achieved the rank of general with the U.S. Army and was the first African-American chairman of the Joint Chiefs of Staff and secretary of state. Powell started his military career in ROTC.

GENERAL COLIN POWELL

The son of Jamaican parents, Colin Powell was born on April 5, 1937, in New York City. He joined the ROTC program while studying at City College of New York in the 1950s, and was commissioned a second lieutenant in the Army at his graduation in 1958.

In the next years Powell's military career sent him to a wide variety of locations in the United States and overseas, including Germany, Vietnam (1962–1963 and 1968–1970), and South Korea (1973–1975). In his assignments he served in various command roles and rose steadily in rank, returning to Germany in the mid-1970s as a lieutenant general.

In 1987 Powell was named deputy assistant for National Security Affairs under President Ronald Reagan. He followed this assignment by working for Reagan, and then for President George Bush, as the National Security Affairs advisor.

In April 1989 Powell was promoted to general under President Bush and served as Commander in Chief of the U.S. Army's Forces Command (FORSCOM). That October, at Bush's appointment, Powell became the first black chairman of the Joint Chiefs of Staff, the highest military position in the Department of Defense.

Powell went on to direct America's participation in the United Nations' operations against Iraqi dictator Saddam Hussein during the Persian Gulf War (1990–1991).

General Powell retired from the Army in 1993 as one of the most respected military leaders in the nation's history, but he has continued his service to the country. In 2001 he became the first African American to serve as secretary of state. Appointed by President George W. Bush, Powell remained in this position through 2005.

CAREERS IN THE U.S. ARMY

West Point cadets celebrate their graduation—and commissions as second lieutenants—by tossing their hats in the air.

WAYS TO SERVE IN THE ARMY

history, languages, and political science. The first female cadets were admitted to West Point in 1976 and, in the twenty-first century, make up approximately 10 to 12 percent of each graduating class.

Admittance to West Point is competitive; there are academic, physical, and medical requirements to become a cadet. Candidates must obtain a nomination from a member of Congress or the Department of the Army. Like any other university, the academy also requires an application, a personal statement, and letters of recommendation.

West Point graduates earn bachelor's degrees and are commissioned as second lieutenants upon graduation, after which they must serve in the Army for a minimum of five years. The U.S. Army provides tuition, room and board, and medical and dental care. Each cadet also receives a stipend to cover uniforms, books, and other personal expenses.

THREE

STARTING LIFE IN UNIFORM

ANY DECISION THAT WILL INVOLVE FOUR or more years of a person's life is a big one. The decision to join the Army is no exception. Some who choose to join are looking for a career, while others want to acquire skills for later civilian use, want to earn the money for college, or simply want to do something that promises adventure and excitement. It can help to talk with family, friends, and even a favorite teacher before making a final decision. Whatever the motive for joining, the first step is enlisting.

ENLISTMENT

Enlistment begins at a local Army recruiting station, where a recruiter will provide an introduction to life in the Army and answer a prospective

All Army enlistees must attend basic training before becoming soldiers. Over the course of nine weeks, men and women learn the basic combat skills that make them effective soldiers.

CAREERS IN THE U.S. ARMY

enlistee's questions. He or she can also help determine what kind of service best suits an enlistee's goals: the regular Army, the Army Reserve, or the National Guard. Once the final decision is made, the enlistee needs to bring a number of documents to the recruiter for review:

1. Birth certificate
2. Social Security card
3. High school diploma and, if applicable, college transcript
4. A list of jobs held and places worked since age sixteen
5. Contact information for four personal references
6. A list of problems with the police, if any, including minor traffic violations
7. A list of places visited outside the United States
8. A list of places lived since age sixteen
9. A medical history, including a list of current medications

Noncitizens need to bring their permanent resident (green card) number and port of entry place and date.

After this information has been discussed with the enlistee, the recruiter will fill out a preliminary medical report that will be reviewed by a doctor. Once cleared, the enlistee is sent to a local military entrance processing station (MEPS), where he or she undergoes a complete physical examination (including hearing and vision testing, blood and urinalysis, and a pregnancy test for women) and takes the Armed Services Vocational Aptitude Battery (ASVAB).

The ASVAB consists of a series of multiple-choice tests. It is not an intelligence (IQ) or academic test; its main pur-

STARTING LIFE IN UNIFORM

pose is to target the military occupational specialty (MOS) best suited for the enlistee based on his or her interests and abilities. The ASVAB tests aptitude in several areas: general science, arithmetic reasoning, electronics, and mechanical comprehension.

After the medical examination and the vocational testing are completed, the enlistee is interviewed by a career classifier, who will advise the enlistee's MOS choice. Finally, with a counselor present, the enlistee will review and sign the enlistment contract.

Upon completion of these steps comes the oath of enlistment ceremony. Enlistees stand before a commissioned officer and recite the oath that makes them members of the U.S. Army:

> I, _____, do solemnly swear (or affirm) that I will support and defend the Constitution of the United States against all enemies, foreign and domestic; that I will bear true faith and allegiance to the same; and that I will obey the orders of the President of the United States and the orders of the officers appointed over me, according to regulations and the Uniform Code of Military Justice.

Not everyone who has taken the oath of enlistment proceeds immediately to basic training; some take advantage of the Army's Delayed Entry Program (DEP), which allows an

CAREERS IN THE U.S. ARMY

enlistee to wait as long as a year before reporting for duty. After the enlistment ceremony, people in the program return to school, work, or family, business, or personal matters. Even though their lives as civilians continue, they are still in the Army and must report for duty at the agreed-upon time.

Trainees maneuver through an obstacle course. BCT features obstacle courses that test the physical and mental skills of trainees and give them confidence in those skills.

STARTING LIFE IN UNIFORM

BASIC COMBAT TRAINING

From the enlistment station, new recruits are sent to basic combat training (BCT), or boot camp, a nine-week period of instruction that consists of both field and classroom training. Basic training is held at Fort Benning (Georgia), Fort Jackson (South Carolina), Fort Knox (Kentucky), Fort McClellan (Alabama), and Fort Sill (Oklahoma). A new recruit is assigned to a BCT location depending on his or her MOS. Even though each MOS has a specialized program of instruction (POI), most of BCT teaches recruits the basic skills to make them effective soldiers.

Before reporting for BCT, cadets should familiarize themselves with The Soldier's Creed, the Army General Orders, the military code of conduct, and the Soldier's Code. It is also helpful to physically prepare for training, which will include marches with full backpacks and an array of strength and conditioning exercises.

The Army also has seven core values, which will be drilled into cadets during BCT: loyalty, duty, respect, selfless service, honor, integrity, personal courage (LDRSHIP). These values are meant to guide every aspect of a soldier's life.

WEEK ONE

The first week of BCT introduces trainees to the core values. The first physical fitness test (PFT) is administered and recruits are taught how to march and prepare their barracks for inspection, they practice drill and ceremony, and they

CAREERS IN THE U.S. ARMY

learn the Military Justice System. Week one also includes instruction in M16 disassembly, reassembly, cleaning, and sighting. Throughout BCT, rifle and marksmanship training will include sessions on aiming and firing techniques, such as proper breathing and trigger squeeze; range safety measures; single- and multiple-target practice; and weapon maintenance.

WEEK TWO

Unarmed combat skills and first aid are taught during the second week of BCT, along with land navigation and map reading. These are all basic skills that every soldier needs to have. Trainees rappel from the 30-foot (9-m) Victory Tower as part of a confidence exercise. The week also emphasizes the importance of loyalty in the Army.

WEEK THREE

Marksmanship and bayonet training, using the M16 rifle, is part of the third week. Trainees take courses in U.S. Army history and the value of duty, learn tactics for defense from chemical attack, and continue their physical training regimen.

WEEK FOUR

Multiple-target detection is added to marksmanship training during week four, and trainees take their second PFT, which demonstrates the progress the new recruits have made. Trainees also learn the Army value of respect.

STARTING LIFE IN UNIFORM

The Warrior Transition Course is for men and women joining the Army after service with another branch of the military. Here, a drill sergeant briefs Air Force and Navy members on Army techniques before a field training exercise at Fort Knox, Kentucky.

WEEK FIVE

During the fifth week of BCT soldiers are awarded badges that designate them as marksmen, sharpshooters, or experts, depending on their performance in a marksmanship exercise. They also learn how the U.S. Army has embodied the value of selfless service throughout its history.

WEEK SIX

Soldiers take the third PFT during week six. They are also introduced to a variety of weapons used by the Army, learn defensive live-fire and tactical movement techniques, and study why honor is an Army value.

WOMEN IN THE ARMY

American women have served with the Army since the Revolutionary War. Mary Ludwig Hays, who followed her husband into service, was nicknamed Molly Pitcher because she carried pitchers of water to American soldiers during the 1778 Battle of Monmouth. When her husband fell in battle, Molly took his place manning the cannon. General George Washington issued her a warrant as a noncommissioned officer for her heroism. Women participated in the Civil War, too, serving as nurses and laundry workers, though some disguised themselves as men and fought.

During World War I, approximately 21,000 women served in the nurse corps of the Army and Navy, while more worked as office personnel. More than 350,000 women served the branches of the military in

World War II. Most worked in medical or administrative fields, but some filled positions as pilots (ferrying planes to bases), truck drivers, mechanics, and gunnery instructors.

In 1942 Congress passed a bill that established the Women's Army Auxiliary Corps (WAAC), giving women an official place within the military; the term *auxiliary* was dropped two years later. Similar groups were established in the other military branches: WAVES (Navy Reserve's Women Accepted for Voluntary Emergency Service), WASP (Women Air Service Pilots), SPARS (U.S. Coast Guard Women's Reserve), and the U.S. Marine Corps Women's Reserve.

WACs served in every theater, filling every noncombatant position, during WWII. General Douglas MacArthur said the WACs worked harder and complained less than men. However, women were still not considered full-time military personnel and, except for nurses, most of the 150,000 women who served left the WAC at the war's end.

In 1948 Congress passed the Women's Armed Services Integration Act. The measure codified the position of women in the military. Like men, they could hold regular military ranks and receive the privileges that came with rank. Limitations were placed on enlistment and promotion, however, and they were barred from combat duty.

Women's role in the military continued to grow. They served in Korea, Vietnam, the Persian Gulf, and Panama. Thanks to a number of court rulings, female officers won the right to command units composed of both men and women, the separate training of males and females came to an end, and the financial entitlements for dependents were made the same for both men and women in the service.

In 1976 women were admitted to West Point and, in 1978, Congress disbanded the Women's Army Corps as a separate entity. Now, with the exception of combat units, men and women serve as equals in the Army.

Left: SGT Nicola Hall (*left*) of the 21st Military Police Company and CPL Jill Osowski, with the 972nd MP Company of the Massachusetts National Guard, on patrol duty in southern Afghanistan. In the fall of 2002, Hall and Osowski were two of the three female MPs assigned to infantry patrol missions.

CAREERS IN THE U.S. ARMY

WEEK SEVEN

During the seventh week of BCT soldiers must pass the final PFT; those who do not must undergo extra physical conditioning before graduating boot camp. Recruits must negotiate the twenty-four–obstacle Confidence Course, which, as its name suggests, is meant to instill confidence in a soldier's mental and physical abilities. It also serves as preparation for challenges they might face as soldiers in the field. In the classroom, the recruits are introduced to the Army's legacy of integrity, another core value.

WEEK EIGHT

During week eight recruits undergo a three-day field test called the Warrior Field Training Exercise (FTX), in which they must apply all the skills they have learned during BCT. Warrior field training includes a long march and team exercises, such as night infiltration.

WEEK NINE

By the ninth and final week of BCT, recruits have the confidence and training to move forward in their careers with the Army. There is a ceremony, which friends and family may attend, marking the beginning of life as soldiers for the graduates.

ON-DUTY TRAINING

After successfully completing BCT soldiers move on to advanced individual training (AIT). The Army offers AIT

STARTING LIFE IN UNIFORM

courses in more than 150 areas for active-duty soldiers and more than 120 areas for men and women with the Reserve or the National Guard.

AIT courses are usually between seven and nine weeks long, though training can last up to a year for highly specialized areas. Soldiers receive a combination of classroom and field training to prepare them for their MOS.

SPC Oscar Osorio is a parachute rigger with the 647th Quartermaster Detachment. The unit airdrops supplies to ground troops. Here, Osorio works aboard a C-130 Hercules attaching the parachute activation cord before sending the bundle to the ground.

CAREERS IN THE U.S. ARMY

There are specialties within each of the Army's branches. Combat MOSs, which are not open to women because they involve combat-zone placement, include field artillery surveyor and armor crewman. The Transportation Corps has MOSs including motor vehicle mechanic and aircraft mechanic. In the medical field, enlisted soldiers can work as health-care, laboratory, or nursing technicians. The administrative branch offers specialized work in financial management and public affairs. For soldiers in the mechanical, electrical, and electronic branches, MOSs include heavy construction equipment operator, aircraft electrician, motor transport operator, technical engineer, and telecommunications operator/maintainer.

Once a soldier has completed AIT, he or she can take courses that will facilitate promotions. Such leadership training is recommended for men and women planning on a military career. Most rank promotions require courses that provide the necessary training so a soldier can fulfill his or her duties as a leader:

WARRIOR LEADER COURSE (WLC) is for soldiers seeking promotion to the rank of sergeant and is usually the first leadership course an enlisted soldier will take.

BASIC NONCOMMISSIONED OFFICER COURSE (BNCOC) provides leadership training for a variety of jobs and may lead to the promotion to staff sergeant.

STARTING LIFE IN UNIFORM

ADVANCED NONCOMMISSIONED OFFICER COURSE (ANCOC) provides training for sergeants first class and staff sergeants ready for promotion.

FIRST SERGEANT ACADEMY prepares sergeants first class and master sergeants for promotion to first sergeant of a company, battery, or troop.

SERGEANTS MAJOR ACADEMY trains sergeants major for work at the battalion command level.

FOUR

THE CHAIN OF COMMAND

EVERY ENLISTED SOLDIER AND OFFICER IS part of the chain of command, the organizational arrangement along which orders are passed. It enables the Army to function quickly and decisively in any situation. At the top is the president of the United States, then the Chief of Staff of the Army, followed by the top-ranked commissioned officers, other commissioned and noncommissioned officers, and enlisted soldiers; at the bottom of the chain are the new recruits.

The chain of command applies to every group of soldiers, no matter where they are or what the objective is. Soldiers with rank and experience are in charge and are responsible for giving orders, which are then passed along the chain until it is received by the soldiers who will execute the task.

During urban terrain combat training, PFC Mathew Pennington stays alert and keeps his weapon ready as his team's rear guard.

CAREERS IN THE U.S. ARMY

While at Camp New York in Kuwait, the 2nd Brigade, 3rd Infantry Division practices tactics with live weapons. Constant training and drilling are part of a soldier's daily regimen, particularly for units deployed to combat areas.

If two soldiers have been separated from their unit, the soldier with the higher rank or with more experience is in command.

THE BASIC UNITS

The Army is organized into operational units for optimal chain-of-command functioning:

SQUAD

A squad consists of four to ten soldiers and is headed by a staff sergeant, sergeant, or corporal. Except for units assigned to

THE CHAIN OF COMMAND

specific duties, this is the smallest organized unit in the Army. The smallest armor unit is called a section, not a squad, and consists of two vehicles, each with a four-man crew.

PLATOON

A platoon is made up of sixteen to forty-four soldiers (three to four squads), usually commanded by a first or second lieutenant. An infantry platoon is made up of three squads, while a tank platoon consists of four tanks.

COMPANY

There are between 100 and 130 soldiers (three to five platoons) in a company, which is led by a captain. A company is tactical and sized to function on the battlefield, so there can be as few as sixty soldiers. A company-sized force is called a troop in a ground or air cavalry unit, and a battery in a field or air defense artillery unit.

BATTALION

A battalion averages between 500 and 600 soldiers, though it can range from as small as 300 to as large as 1,000 (three to six companies). Battalions are commanded by a lieutenant colonel and are tactically and administratively self-sufficient. An armored or air cavalry unit of equal size is known as a squadron. A battalion task force is a battalion with an additional company attached to enhance mission capabilities.

CAREERS IN THE U.S. ARMY

BRIGADE

Brigades range in size from 1,500 to 5,000 soldiers (three or more battalions) and are commanded by a colonel or a brigadier general. An armored cavalry brigade is called a regiment and a Ranger or Special Forces brigade is called a group.

DIVISION

A division is a combination of infantry, artillery, and armored units, consisting of a total of 10,000 to 18,000 soldiers (three brigades). It is commanded by a major general

The 602nd Area Support Medical Company returns after a year of service in the Middle East. Medics with the 602nd treated more than 22,000 soldiers and detainees and trained local groups in different medical practices during the company's tour of duty.

THE CHAIN OF COMMAND

who engages in sustained battles and is responsible for major tactical operations. Divisions are numbered and categorized as light infantry, mechanized infantry, armor, airborne, or air assault (e.g., 1st Airborne).

CORPS

A corps is a force of 20,000 to 40,000 soldiers (two to five divisions), in addition to support personnel, that is commanded by a lieutenant general. The U.S. Army currently maintains four corps—three are headquartered in the United States and one in Germany.

FIELD ARMY

A field army, the largest unit within the Army, is made up of two to five corps composed of various units as required for successful action. It is commanded by a general.

ENLISTED SOLDIERS

Few things in the life of a soldier have more daily impact than rank, and rank is directly linked to pay. A rank is a title, such as lieutenant. Most ranks correspond to pay grades, or levels, which are designated alphanumerically. The nine Army pay grades for enlisted personnel begin with the letter E.

The ranks of Private, Private Second Class, and Private First Class are pay grades E-1 through E-3, respectively. New recruits begin BCT as privates. All privates must carry out orders and assigned tasks to the best of their ability.

CAREERS IN THE U.S. ARMY

Promotion to the rank of Specialist (E-4) generally requires a minimum of two years of service and completion of a training class to prepare specialists for managing privates.

A Corporal (E-4) is the lowest noncommissioned officer (NCO) rank. NCOs are enlisted soldiers who have shown themselves to have command capabilities. A commissioned officer usually has at least a college degree and has undergone special training; he or she delegates responsibility to NCOs. Even though specialists and corporals are in the same pay grade, corporals outrank the specialists as NCOs and serve as leaders for small units.

The NCO ranks of Sergeant (E-5), Staff Sergeant (E-6), and Sergeant First Class (E-7) entail significant leadership responsibilities. Sergeants usually command squads and, because they supervise and advise their soldiers daily, are recognized as one of the most influential ranks. Staff sergeants develop and utilize each soldier's potential while sergeants first class, who have fifteen to eighteen years of experience, serve as advisors to commissioned officers leading a platoon.

The final two pay grades include the highest-ranking NCOs: Master Sergeant (E-8), First Sergeant (E-8), Sergeant Major (E-9), and Command Sergeant Major (E-9). To become senior NCOs soldiers must have technical expertise in their field, be able to handle extensive administrative duties, and provide leadership and support to the men and women in their command.

THE CHAIN OF COMMAND

The highest rank that an enlisted soldier can achieve is that of Sergeant Major of the Army (E-9). Very few people ever achieve this rank. His or her job is to oversee all non-commissioned officers and to advise and consult with the Chief of Staff of the Army (a four-star general) and the other highest-ranking commissioned officers in matters pertaining to enlisted personnel. Only one Sergeant Major of the Army serves at a time.

ARMY OFFICERS

Any active or Reserve soldier who wishes to become an officer may apply for admission to the Army's Officer Candidate School (OCS), which provides management opportunities in sixteen career fields. All men and women with a bachelor's degree or higher from an accredited university are eligible for acceptance.

The twelve-week course, held at Fort Benning (Georgia), combines classroom learning with field training to develop leadership skills. OCS is divided into two phases. During phase one, candidates are taught basic leadership skills and they face physical and mental challenges to prepare them for their roles as commissioned officers. The second phase is an eighteen-day training mission that tests the candidates' skills and abilities—both as a leader and on a team—in a field environment.

Candidates that successfully complete the OCS program of instruction are commissioned as second lieu-

ARMY RANK INSIGNIA

ENLISTED RANKS

Badges on a soldier's uniform indicate his or her rank. In the Army, ranks are designated by various arrangements of stripes and diamonds.

Private (PVT): no insignia

Private Second Class (PV2)

Private First Class (PFC)

Specialist (SPC)

Corporal (CPL)

Sergeant (SGT)

Staff Sergeant (SSG)

Sergeant First Class (SFC)

Master Sergeant (MSG)

First Sergeant (1SG)

Sergeant Major (SGM)

Command Sergeant Major (CSM)

Sergeant Major of the Army (SMA)

OFFICERS

Gold and silver bars, leaves, stars, and even an eagle are used in the rank insignia worn by officers in the Army.

Second Lieutenant (2LT)

First Lieutenant (1LT)

Captain (CPT)

Major (MAJ)

Lieutenant Colonel (LTC)

Colonel (COL)

Brigadier General (BG)

Major General (MG)

Lieutenant General (LTG)

General (GEN)

General of the Army (GA)

WARRANT OFFICERS

Warrant Officer (WO1)

Chief Warrant Officer (CW2)

Chief Warrant Officer (CW3)

Chief Warrant Officer (CW4)

Chief Warrant Officer (CW5)

CAREERS IN THE U.S. ARMY

Kenneth Preston was promoted to Sergeant Major at the Pentagon in 2004. Army Chief of Staff GEN Peter Schoomaker and Preston's wife, Karen, pin new shoulder boards on Preston at the formal swearing-in ceremony.

THE CHAIN OF COMMAND

tenants in the Army. Commissioned Army officers are classified into ten pay grades, designated by the letter O, and eleven ranks. Officers in pay grades O-1 to O-3 are called company grade officers, those in grades O-4 to O-6 are field grade officers, and those classified as O-7 and higher are general officers. Commissioned officers hold presidential appointments that are confirmed by the Senate.

Warrant officers are specialists or trainers in a given field of expertise. They concentrate on advancing in that field rather than seeking advancement via command or staff positions. The five warrant officer pay grades are designated by the letter W.

FIVE

SALARY AND BENEFITS

THERE ARE FINANCIAL, EDUCATIONAL, and personal benefits available to members of the U.S. Army. The benefits for full-time soldiers and soldiers with the Reserve and the National Guard are slightly different.

BENEFITS

ENLISTED ACTIVE DUTY

1. Full-time salary
2. Thirty days paid vacation annually
3. Retirement income plus savings program
4. Free medical, dental, and hospital care (includes family members, if married)
5. Low-cost post exchange (PX) (department store) and commissary (grocery store) privileges
6. Low-cost life insurance

Soldiers with the 1st Battalion, 1st Special Operations Airborne Unit, practice jumps out of a Sea Knight helicopter. ARSOF units have the most challenging jobs and training in the U.S. Army.

CAREERS IN THE U.S. ARMY

7. Extra income includes allowances for subsistence housing and uniforms

RESERVE

1. Part-time salary
2. Full-time pay and allowance for meals and housing during the two-week annual training period
3. Health care for injury or illness during active duty or training periods
4. Low-cost life insurance
5. PX and commissary privileges
6. Retirement program

NATIONAL GUARD

1. Part-time salary
2. Full-time pay and allowance for meals and housing during the two-week annual training period
3. State benefits and retirement plan
4. Low-cost life insurance

SALARY AND SPECIAL PAY

Pay for all members of the Army, enlisted personnel as well as officers, increases with each rank or grade promotion. Promotions in the lower enlisted grades usually happen quickly. Salaries also reflect increases in the cost of living allowance (COLA).

SALARY AND BENEFITS

SGM Tory Hendrieth describes the training, educational, and career opportunities the Army offers to high school freshman Danie Foster.

In addition to the base salary, compensation is given for work that requires extra duty, greater responsibilities, or hazardous working conditions. Certain highly selective units with the Army, such as the Green Berets, receive extra pay. A soldier is also paid for serving in areas where the living conditions are below those at U.S. bases.

EDUCATION

The Army provides its soldiers—active duty, Reserve, and National Guard—with the facilities and financial means to improve their lives and careers by continuing their educa-

CAREERS IN THE U.S. ARMY

tion. Courses for all Army personnel are available at colleges near duty stations and as correspondence or online courses for those serving in isolated areas. The Army, along with the other military branches, offers programs to soldiers seeking financial aid and career assistance.

EARNING A COLLEGE DEGREE

The U.S. Army offers the Concurrent Admissions Program (CONAP) as an incentive to enlistees who also want to obtain a college degree. There are more than 1,800 colleges and universities that recognize credits earned during a soldier's military training. The Army has partnerships with these establishments, enabling soldiers to take classes and work toward a degree during or after their military service.

Soldiers can also continue their education while on base or abroad. Most Army bases have satellite campuses of local universities so soldiers can take college courses. Virtual classes through eArmyU provide soldiers with the opportunity to earn a degree from an accredited college or university in more than one hundred fields of study. Both programs enable soldiers to work toward an associate's, bachelor's, or master's degree.

THE MONTGOMERY GI BILL AND
THE ARMY COLLEGE FUND

The Montgomery GI Bill (MGIB) and the Army College Fund (ACF) are generously endowed government programs

SALARY AND BENEFITS

ROTC cadet Larry Baca uses an iPod while doing schoolwork. Podcasting technology is already used by the U.S. Army's websites. Baca, a student at New Mexico State University, is demonstrating how podcasting could be used by personnel serving in the field who wish to take academic courses.

WARRIOR ETHOS

The Warrior Ethos is soldier's promise to him- or herself and to all comrades:

I will always place the mission first.

I will never accept defeat.

I will never quit.

I will never leave a fallen comrade.

that help Army personnel attain their civilian education or vocational training goals.

Soldiers on active duty, as well as certain members of the Reserve, are eligible to apply for these programs, which can help finance a college education. Active-duty soldiers who sign up for the MGIB and the ACF must contribute $100 each month during the first year of service to receive more than $70,000 toward tuition. Soldiers with the Army Reserve or ARNG who accept a critical skilled position can qualify for a Reserve or ARNG MGIB Kicker of up to approximately $24,000.

The Army College Loan Repayment Program is an option for soldiers who are paying off student loans. Soldiers must enlist for full-time active duty for at least three years, or for six years of Reserve duty, to qualify. The ARNG also offers student loan repayment assistance.

SALARY AND BENEFITS

ROTC cadets in their uniforms line up and salute. The Army offers ROTC scholarships to applicants of high academic standing.

ROTC SCHOLARSHIPS

The ROTC program offers two- and four-year scholarships to college students who want to be commissioned in the Army at graduation.

Scholarships are awarded based on merit and the program has strict requirements. Good grades, high class ranking, good college entrance exam results, and extracurricular activities are important factors.

Tuition, educational costs (such as textbooks), uniforms, and a subsistence allowance are funded by a ROTC scholar-

CAREERS IN THE U.S. ARMY

SGT Heriberto Vargas, CPL Jenny Cline, SMA Kenneth O. Preston, SPC Jessica Carpenter, and 1SG Charles Orange swear in a group of high school graduates who have signed up for the Army's Delayed Entry Program.

SALARY AND BENEFITS

ship. As with all ROTC cadets, scholarship recipients must fulfill an eight-year service obligation.

BE ALL THAT YOU CAN BE

Service in the active-duty Army, the Army Reserve, and the National Guard are all equally admirable and can provide great opportunities and lead to a satisfying career. Information on service in the Navy, the Air Force, the Marine Corps, and the Coast Guard is available in the other books in this series, which explain how each branch provides work, adventure, and experience in a wide variety of activities and fields.

ACRONYM GLOSSARY

ACF	Army College Fund
ACS	Artillery computer systems
AIT	Advanced Individual Training
AMEDD	Army Medical Department
ANCOC	Advanced Noncommissioned Officer course
ARNG	Army National Guard
ARSOF	Army Special Operations Forces
ASVAB	Armed Services Vocational Aptitude Battery
BCT	Basic Combat Training
BNCOC	Basic Noncommissioned Officer course
COLA	Cost of living allowance
E	Enlisted, in pay grade designation
FORSCOM	Forces Command
FTX	Field training exercise
GI	Government issue
JAG	Judge Advocate General's Corps
MEPS	Military Entrance Processing Station
MGIB	Montgomery GI Bill
MI	Military Intelligence
MLRS	Multiple-launch rocket system
MOS	Military Occupational Specialty
MP	Military Police
NBC	Nuclear, biological, and chemical
NCO	Noncommissioned officer
O	Officer, in pay grade designation
OCS	Officer Candidate School
POI	Program of instruction
PX	Post exchange; also called base exchange (BX)
ROTC	Reserve Officers Training Corps
W	Warrant officer, in pay grade designation
WAC	Women's Army Corps; originally WAAC
WLC	Warrior Leader course

FURTHER INFORMATION

WEBSITES

The website of the U.S. Army
www.army.mil

The website of the U.S. Army Reserve
www.armyreserve.army.mil/ARWEB

The website of the U.S. Army for new and potential recruits
www.goarmy.com

The website of the U.S. Army ROTC program
www.goarmy.com/rotc

The website of the National Guard
www.ngb.army.mil

The website of the U.S. Military Academy
www.usma.edu

SELECTED BIBLIOGRAPHY

Axelrod, Alan, and Charles Phillips. *Macmillan Dictionary of Military Biography*. New York: Macmillan, 1998.

Brookhiser, Richard. *Founding Father: Rediscovering George Washington*. New York: The Free Press/Simon & Schuster, 1996.

Chambers, John Whiteclay, II, ed. *The Oxford Companion to American Military History*. New York: Oxford University Press, 1999.

Holmes, Richard, ed. *The Oxford Companion to Military History*. New York: Oxford University Press, 2001.

INDEX

Page numbers in **boldface** are illustrations, tables, and charts.

Abdon, Hardenio, **21**
active duty, 8, 28
Adjutant General Corps, 19
Advanced Individual Training (AIT), 50–52
Advanced Noncommissioned Officer course (ANCOC), 53
Air Defense Artillery, 12
Air National Guard (ANG), 32
Armed Services Vocational Aptitude Battery (ASVAB), 42–43
Armor, 14
Army Aviation, 12
Army College Fund (ACF), 70, 72
Army College Loan Repayment Program, 72
Army Medical Department (AMEDD), 23–25
Army National Guard (ARNG), **27**, 31–32 , **31**
Army officers, 61, 63, 65
Army Rangers, 25
Army Reserve, 8, 28, 30

Baca, Larry, **71**
basic combat training, **41**, **44**, 45–47, 50
Basic Noncommissioned Officer course (BNCOC), 52
battalion, 57
Bodle, Nathan, **31**
branches of the Army, 10–25
brigade, 58
Brown, Michael, **31**

Carpenter, Jessica, **74**
chain of command, 54, 56–61, 65

Chaplains Corps, 23
Chatman, Donald, **7**
Chemical Corps, 17
Cline, Jenny, **74**
Combat Arms branches, 12–17
Combat Service Support, 19–20, 23
Combat Support Arms, 17–19
company, 57, **58**
Concurrent Admissions Program (CONAP), 70
Confidence Course, 50
Continental army, 6
corps, 59
Corps of Engineers, 14

Delayed Entry Program (DEP), 43–44, **74**
Delta Force, 25
dime-and-washer exercise, 7, **7**
division, 58–59
drill instructors, 13

education, 69–70, **71**, 72–73, 75
enlisted ranks, 62
enlisted soldiers, 59–61
enlistment
procedure, 40, 42–44
reasons for, 8–9
requirements, 26, 28

field army, 59
Field Artillery, 16
Finance Corps, 19–20
First Sergeant Academy, 53
Foster, Danie, **69**

Green Berets, 25

Hall, Nicola, **48**
Hendrieth, Tory, **69**

howitzer, **15**, 16

Infantry, 17, **27**, **56**
insignia, Army rank, 62–63, **62–63**

Judge Advocate General's Corps
    (JAG), 24

M16 rifles, **11**, 16, **16**, 17
Military Entrance Processing
    Station (MEPS), 42
Military Intelligence Corps, 18
Military Police Corps, 18, **21**, **48**
Montgomery GI Bill (MGIB), 70, 72
mortars, 16, 22

National Guard, 8, **27**, 31–32, **31**

on-duty training, 50–53, **56**
Orange, Charles, **74**
Ordnance Corps, 20
Osorio, Oscar, **51**
Osowski, Jill, **48**

Pennington, Mathew, **55**
platoon, 57
Powell, Colin, **36**, 37
Preston, Karen, **64**
Preston, Kenneth, **64**, **74**
promotions, **64**, 68

Quartermaster Corps, 20, 23, **51**

reenlistment, **29**
Reserve Officers Training Corps
    (ROTC), 32–35, **33**, **71**, 73, **73**,
    75
retirement, 28
Revolutionary War, 6
Rex, MP canine, **21**

Rowland, Lindsey, **33**

salary and benefits, 59–60, 65, 66,
    68–70, 72–73, 75
scholarships, 34, 73, 75
Schoomaker, Peter, **64**
Sergeants Major Academy, 53
Signal Corps, 18–19
Special Branches, 23–25
Special Forces, 25
Special Operations Forces, 24–25,
    24, **66**
squad, 56–57
Swankie, John, **24**

Transportation Corps, 23

U.S. Military Academy, 35, 39

Vargas, Heriberto, **74**
von Steuben, Friedrich Wilheim,
    13, **13**

warrant officers, 63, 65
Warrior Ethos, 72
Warrior Field Training Exercise
    (FTX), 50
Warrior Leader Course (WLC), 52
Warrior Transition Course, 47, **47**
Washington, George, 6
weapons terminology, 22
West Point cadets, **38**
West Point Military Academy, 35, 39
women in the Army, 48–49, **48**

ABOUT THE AUTHOR

EDWARD F. DOLAN is the author of more than 120 published nonfiction books. His most recent book for Marshall Cavendish Benchmark is *George Washington* in the series Presidents and Their Times. Mr. Dolan is a California native and currently resides near San Francisco.